Faith and Freedom

SpeakUp Conference

Compiled by

Living Parables of Central Florida

Faith and Freedom

Volume 2

Copyright © 2018 Living Parables of Central Florida, Inc.

All rights reserved.

ISBN: 978-1-945975-29-5

Published by EA Books Publishing a division of
Living Parables of Central Florida, Inc. a 501c3
EABooksPublishing.com

Living Parables of Central Florida, a 501c3

ACKNOWLEDGMENTS

We'd like to thank Carol Kent and Bonnie Emmorey of the SpeakUp Conference for encouraging and equipping writers and speakers for the glory of the Kingdom of God. We wish to thank Cheri Cowell and her wonderful team at EABooks Publishing for giving us this opportunity. We thank our many friends and family for supporting us in our writing dreams. And most importantly, we want to thank our Lord and Savior Jesus Christ for His gifts—may this book bring you the honor and glory you deserve.

TABLE OF CONTENTS

Acknowledgements

Frames of Faith   1
    Julie Pluger

Fearless Beauty Brings Freedom   5
    Victoria Ann

Know Faith — Know Freedom   9
    Sheila Qualls

Entrusted   13
    Sheri Hawley

Assigned by Design   17
    Janice Ayers Davis

See Free   21
    Gia Layne Wood

A Moment of Failure   27
    Sarah Raines

Serenade My Soul with Wonder   31
    W. Ruth Esau

Let Your Daughters Live   35
    Alissa Joy Sande

Goodbye Food, Hello Jesus   39
    Dana Remisovsky

Only Faith in Jesus Spells Freedom   43
    Robert Harmon

Forgiven and Free   47
Deedy Tripp

She Loves Jesus and America Too   51
Jenny Maass Klobuchar

Set Free   55
Barbara Riffenburg

The Freedom of Faith   57
Destiny Whitfield

Sweet Freedom   59
Carol Ensminger

Lord of All   63
Linda Coulson

My Beloved Child   67
Stacy Robert

Breaking Free   71
Dawn Lynn Mann

Gifts of Faith from My Heart Tree   75
Dyann Shepard

Living Parables of Central Florida   79

Faith and Freedom

Frames of Faith

by Julie Pluger

Love, peace, joy — how do we describe them? We can't see them. We know their presence or absence in our lives. We feel them. When I think of Faith and Freedom, I think of living securely, in the presence of God's love, peace, and joy. With complete faith in God, our hearts are free to relax in His power and promises. At a time when disappointment enveloped me, visualizing God at work in my life enabled me to exit the sadness. Picturing the results of trusting God encouraged me to rest completely in His ability to handle everything concerning me.

During the time I worked as a photographer, I saw much of the world through a camera lens. Smiling faces, colorful flowers, landscapes; I loved framing pictures of people and places. When hardship tested me, my experiences and photos rendered something interesting that strengthened my walk of faith. Slowly, I began to see God's invisible qualities in His beautiful creation. The physical existence of nature gave form to abstract ideas like love, peace, and joy. Eventually, I began to grasp a greater understanding of God's love and power. One day, while considering how His love washed over me, His peace surrounded me. Instead of what I saw in my lens giving me joy, His joy framed my life and my focus changed.

I quit hoping for things to be different. Hope was now something I put in God. Oh, I lost ground for sure, but eventually, I quit fighting it. I surrendered my plan to God's will, and anxiety lost its grip. Peace took over — Joy moved in. Love filled the cracks, and my desire to define happiness through people, places, and things, gave way to finding lasting satisfaction in the un-changing qualities of God.

When we trust His presence in our lives, we reside in His love. We're calm in His care, joyfully free. God wants us to trust Him. He is pleased when our hearts rest on Him. Letting go of worldly cares that hold us captive, opens our hearts for more of His Holy Spirit. When we surrender to His will, we become far more than we ever imagined. We become a portrait of His workmanship.

Do you have complete faith in the God of the Bible? Trust Him completely, and let freedom sing!

Your love is like a waterfall, pouring down on me.

I sit on the rock, and cool water splashes over me.

I don't want to leave. I see your power. I feel your strength. I am refreshed.

Lord, let your love flow through me. Like water over the rocks, smooth me.

Wash every part of my soul. Fix the cracks and mend the holes. Take all of my impurities.

Your love is my guarantee.

I will trust you. I will trust you. I will trust you.

Your peace is like a group of trees, standing straight and tall.

The sun is shining in, and it's not dark at all.

I don't want to leave. I see your power. I feel your strength. I am safe.

Lord, let your peace surround me. Like the deep roots of these trees, ground me.

Calm every anxious heartbeat, secure me in your retreat.

When my courage multiplies, your peace is the reason why.

I will trust you. I will trust you. I will trust you.

Your joy is like a gentle breeze by the ocean shore.

Every breath I take makes me smile more.

I don't want to leave. I see your power. I feel your strength. I am alive.

Lord, let your breath come to me. Like the waves break on the shore, pursue me.

Renew me inside out. You trade me faith for doubt. My lasting joy will be –

Only when I totally trust you.

I will trust you. I will trust you. I will trust you.

Prayer:
    Dear God, will you please help me trust you? When I feel tempted to fret will you remind me of Your Faithfulness? I put everything in your powerful, but very tender hands. Secure me in your love. Ground me in your Word. Calm my fear. Grant me a faithful heart that is always turned toward you. I trust you completely. Thank-You for the freedom that comes with faith in you.

"Blessed are all they that put their trust in him" *(Psalm 2:12:B KJV).*

"For we are His workmanship, created in Christ Jesus unto good works, which God hath before ordained that we should walk in them" *(Ephesians 2:10 KJV).*

Julie is a musician, photographer, and singer/songwriter. Her motto, and favorite Bible verse is "Rejoice in the LORD Always." She loves cheering people toward God through praise and worship. Her richest inspiration is the Word of God. Her greatest joy is admiring Jesus and helping others admire Him, too.

Fearless Beauty Brings Freedom

Victoria Ann

"Wives, in the same way submit yourselves to your own husbands so that, if any of them do not believe the word, they may be won over without words by the behavior of their wives, when they see the purity and reverence of your lives. Your beauty should not come from outward adornment, such as elaborate hairstyles and the wearing of gold jewelry or fine clothes. Rather, it should be that of your inner self, the unfading beauty of a gentle and quiet spirit, which is of great worth in God's sight. For this is the way the holy women of the past who put their hope in God used to adorn themselves. They submitted themselves to their own husbands, like Sarah, who obeyed Abraham and called him her lord. You are her daughters if you do what is right and do not give way to fear" (1 Peter 3.1-6 NIV)

As a Christian woman living in western society, I often find myself in conflict. The world around me whispers (and sometimes shouts!) that I should be independent, self-sufficient, and beautiful. There is an invisible and impossibly high bar for women. I am told that if I achieve these standards I can be in control and valued. I'll be honest, these promises speak straight to my humanness and fleshly desires to guide my own destiny and be important. But I've learned, they are false promises. Striving for these standards undermines joy by creating an environment of self-focus and comparison that traps a woman in a cycle of bondage. She becomes so focused on herself that she falls prey to the lie

"It's all about me." What gets lost or simply neglected is that her actual identity, source of beauty, and value are rooted in Christ.

In stark contrast to our culture, Peter's words in the New Testament set forth a realistic, freeing vision of biblical womanhood. He describes the need for submission to authority, leaning into our inner beauty, and having a gentle and quiet spirit. As we lean into Christ and His grace and sufficiency, we aren't relying on ourselves, or our beauty, or our personalities to get things done. We are not trying to be the best version of ourselves. We are leaning into Christlikeness and the strength that only comes from the One who did it perfect for us.

"Wait," you might say, "how does submission bring me freedom?" I know, it sounds restrictive and raises all kinds of emotions for women, especially when we look through our cultural lens. But the truth is, submission provides protection and not just for women. The context of Peter's exhortation is for the married woman, yet we all have to submit to authority in our lives. Order and structure is a good thing, whether working for a boss or yielding to laws. In the specific case of a married woman, when I properly align my respect for my husband's authority, I can rest in the fact that I am not navigating this life on my own. The church also falls under Christ's authority (Ephesians 5.23-24) and it rests in the knowledge that He is always with us covering us with protection and direction. In the same way, when a married woman aligns herself under the protection of her husband's guidance, she can rest knowing that the Lord has a specific role that is best for her. Submission gives us true freedom and confidence and forces us to rely on Christ and not ourselves.

Peter goes on to encourage women to lean into our inner beauty, meaning that our source of beauty comes from the inside. It is freeing to know that our outward appearance, which is fleeting, does not define us and does not need to be our focus. I admit that when I first read Peter's words "gentle and quiet," I wondered why, if this was what God expected of me, He would give me a Type A personality with boldness to speak up. But it is not a matter of personality; it is a matter of spirit and character. Peter isn't saying that we are to be weak or cowardly. We are to be humble just like Christ, who relied on God and rested in His Sovereignty and trusted Him. This took a great deal of humility! Peter is exhorting us to reliance on Christ and not ourselves. When we trust the Lord to meet our needs and when we rely on Christ's strength and not our own, we find ourselves acting out of a humble spirit, one that does not have to strive for attention or to get its own way. We all know a Christian woman like this, a woman who knows her worth in Christ and is peaceful and grace-filled. She is inherently beautiful.

These biblical roles raise conflict in a world that constantly bombards us with messages of independence and self-reliance. We buy into these messages out of fear: If I give up my rights, privileges, and control, no one else will look out for me and I will fail. If I am not striving to be valued and seen by others, then I have no purpose or meaning. But in our efforts to soothe these fears with our own actions, we leave ourselves open to sins of pride, vanity, extravagance, and self-centeredness. We worship and rely on ourselves, with all of our limitations and insecurities, more than Christ. Peter encourages women not to give way to this fear. Instead we are to place our confidence in Christ, entrusting Him with our worth, our place in this world, and everything else we value.

In his writings, Peter calls us to a life of submission and humility, to follow Christ even when it is difficult. When we put our faith in Jesus and fully trust that He guards our hearts, we can live out this calling. We can navigate this life without fear, trusting that He has us held in His wings of grace, and we can rest under His umbrella of protection. Ultimately, the beauty of submission and having a gentle and quiet spirit is that it illuminates Jesus and His work on our behalf. This is fearless beauty and the freedom found in following Christ.

Victoria is lover of Jesus, authenticity, coffee, and all things tropical. She considers it a joy to navigate life with her husband where there is never a dull moment with teen boys and Mastiff dogs. She serves at her home church building leaders and ministering to women. www.victoriaannministry.com

Know Faith — Know Freedom

Sheila Qualls

I vowed never to be like my mom. I meant it.

She was mean. The true definition of the word: unpleasant, sometimes even unkind.

Even into my 20's, I wasn't crazy about her. I loved her, but I also tolerated her. She had plenty of reason to be mean. I'm not sure when I began to understand her. I know it was long after having children of my own.

She wanted to give me a better life. She did it the only way she knew how. Although she ruled with an iron fist, she was driven by a justifiable fear and an unbreakable will to succeed. Mom saw a lot of hard times. Maybe more than most. But her unshakeable faith allowed her to rise above her circumstances and take me with her. Her unspoken life lesson to me: Know faith; know freedom.

She was the only child born to a 13 year-old single mother in the 1930's. She grew up during the Depression in rural Oklahoma, literally dirt poor. She dropped out of school in the 8th grade, got married, and started a family. She married a soldier, who took her away from everything and everyone she ever knew. She had to figure it out. By the time she was 21, she'd been married five years and had five kids. She'd eventually have three more. She cared for eight babies using cloth diapers and glass bottles.

Like most moms in those days, she stayed home. But at 21 she was trying to figure out how to feed a houseful of kids and pay the bills. She never wore a wedding ring. It never occurred to me they probably couldn't afford one, and by the time they could, it didn't matter anymore.

My dad was a career soldier, who saw combat in both the Korean and Vietnam Wars. Much of the time, she operated as a single parent. She traveled—in the U.S. and abroad—with eight children in tow, following my dad to new duty stations. She mourned the deaths of President Kennedy and Martin Luther King, Jr. She marveled when men walked on the moon, delighted over her first colored television set, and endured through the Civil Rights Movement.

She was colored, a Negro, Black, and African American, and—as you can imagine—she was called far worse. The mother of eight children and wife to a U.S soldier, still she was refused service at restaurants, denied access to public pools, and turned away from public restrooms in Tennessee. Yet, she understood her freedom wasn't defined by the laws of the land.

She was thrilled every Mother's Day, Christmas or birthday when we gave her a kitchen gadget-a toaster or a can opener. . . or nothing at all. I knew this growing up, but I wasn't mature enough to understand it in context, within the context of her life and how it impacted mine. Life was tough, but she was a mom who showed up.

My life would never be as hard as hers because of the choices she made for me.

She was at every basketball game, every awards ceremony, Girl Scout ceremony, and parents' night. She listened to me read and count. She laughed at my jokes. Even when I didn't believe in myself, she believed in me. I still didn't fully appreciate her even though I cried in her arms after a breakup with my boyfriend in high school. I cried in her arms in the early years in my marriage. It never occurred to me she didn't have earthly arms to comfort her in the early years of her marriage. I didn't appreciate her as I cried in her arms when one of my own children had broken my heart. It had never occurred to me I'd probably broken her heart, too. her feelings never occurred to me at all.

She'd barely had a chance to grow up herself. She was poor and Black, married a Buffalo Soldier (all Black units in the U.S. Army, who helped settle much of the American West until President Truman desegregated the Army in 1948), moved more than eight times in the thirty year-span of his career, sent her own son off to war, and watched her children grow up and grow out of needing her.

Perhaps most importantly, she introduced me to Jesus. She taught me to be a staunch advocate for my children, to love my country, and to stay married for better or for worse. She's been married for 65 years. It wasn't 65 years of bliss, but she stuck it out. She knew what it was like to grow up without a father, and she didn't want that for me. When I was 15, I was in high school, not pregnant, not married. And at 21, I was in college, not raising five kids. I didn't have my first child until I was almost thirty.

I've never worried about putting food on the table or struggled to pay my bills. I've never been denied access to anything. It never occurred to me many of the things I experienced during those years, she was experiencing for the first time, also: A wedding, high school, and college graduations.

Now the corners of her mouth are permanently turned down with age, but I remember that tired woman who got me up in the mornings, taught me the importance of being a lady, and tried to make every Christmas and birthday special. My selfish perspective has changed through the lens of maturity. Now I see a mother's heart whose compassion was sometimes stifled by fear.

I now realize that because of her, I don't have to be the same kind of mom she was.

She might've wanted something different out of life, but she took what she got and made it her dream. And, she realized it. She moved her desires to the back burner and gave me both faith and freedom to be any kind of mom I want to be.

Sheila Qualls translates biblical principles into practical tools to equip women to do marriage better. She gives women an up-close view of her hurt, disappointments, and failures as a wife and the work arounds and cheat sheets she used to experience lasting change. She is a former editor of the Army's award-winning newspaper the Cannoneer and holds a Masters Degree in Human Communication Theory. She blogs as The Not So Excellent Wife. In addition to her blog, you can follow her on Facebook at The Not So Excellent Wife or on Patheos, where she writes a weekly column. You can also find her work the MOPS Blog, Scary Mommy, The Mighty, and Grown and Flown.

Entrusted

Sheri Hawley

Have you ever worked with someone who had an entitlement mindset? A person who felt everyone around owed him or her something? Dealing with co-workers, neighbors, or friends like that can be frustrating.

The summer between my freshman and sophomore years of college, I worked a job that was challenging for me. Somehow, I managed to land a position working at one of the most prestigious clothing stores in my hometown of Pensacola, FL. They must have been desperate for dependable workers because I've never been fashion conscious. This was not a natural fit.

Sam's Style Shop catered to wealthy clients. The customer base was predominantly people ready to spend serious money for quality clothing. One lady came in while I was working and purchased an entire fall wardrobe for her daughter who had just been accepted to Harvard.

I wasn't a natural with design, but I did arrive early and avoided complaining about whatever lowly task was assigned. That's how I soon became a favorite with the manager, Lu. She was both a beautiful fashionista, and a bright businesswoman.

All sales associates worked on commission. We were paid an hourly wage ($2.20 in those days), but the real money for us was in selling entire outfits to the customers. If they looked at a skirt, we quickly produced the matching jacket and a separate blouse. If they came in searching for a more casual look, we suggested multiple colors, prints and even accessories. Fortunately for me, these were usually grouped together making it almost foolproof.

Our job was to place each potential buyer in one of the plush dressing rooms and then not let them leave that mirrored room until they had selected an outfit—hopefully, two or more. Many days my high heels covered several miles as I ran back and forth getting the different sizes, colors, and styles the ladies wanted to try.

Apparently, I was friendly enough to pull in a few customers. And as was already mentioned, the manager was kind to me. But there was one older lady who had worked there for years (I can't even remember her name, so we'll call her Mary).

Mary quickly established that I was NOT to approach any of her regulars. I understood. Her boundary lines were fine with me. The only problem was that she spent most of her time sitting in the break area, and I had no way of knowing which ladies were her patrons.

There were countless times that I would work with a customer, running back and forth for long stretches while they tried every outfit in their size. Finally, when they'd come to the point of a sale, Mary would swoop in and say, "Thanks, Sheri! Madelyn here has been my friend for years. I'll take it from here."

I was young and didn't like correcting anyone older than me, especially not in front of the customer. How was I to combat Mary's smooth technique?

One evening, while helping close up, I sheepishly addressed the problem with Lu. "Oh, Sheri! Mary feels entitled to those sales because she's been here so long. I know it's not fair but she does have seniority. Just try to do the best you can."

Fortunately for me, I knew my time working there was only temporary. But the experience was one I've carried through life. I've watched it repeated in a wide variety of venues. At times people have ranted about young people feeling entitled, but I know from experience that entitlement thinking is a matter of attitude, not age.

Years later, I finally understood that the antidote for feeling entitled is feeling entrusted instead.

In this wonderful country, we've been entrusted with great freedoms. These freedoms were provided for us at great cost to those who have gone before. Remembering this truth keeps us from struggling with the monster of entitlement thinking.

We are not Entitled. We are Entrusted.

We aren't entitled to all the richness of life in this country. Rather, we understand that incredible blessings have been entrusted to us as citizens. The price has been paid. We are both beneficiaries and custodians of incredible opportunity.

God has generously preserved this nation and trusts us to be generous in return. Understanding His great love and lavish mercy causes us to respond with a sense of profound gratitude. We recognize our opportunities and we work toward maximizing them. There is no room for selfishness in a heart that is busy and grateful.

This country owes me nothing. My family and friends owe me nothing. God certainly owes me nothing. However, the freedoms I've been given were given generously and that perspective makes me a thankful woman!

Hopefully, Mary eventually came to understand the great chasm between being *Entitled* and *Entrusted*. I am grateful I've learned this truth and, therefore, I choose to live knowing that every relationship and every blessing in my life has been entrusted to God. I can promise you from experience that if you, too choose to live with this perspective it will make you feel like the wealthiest person around.

You have been entrusted!

Sheri Hawley is wife to one amazing man; mother to three daughters and three sons-in-law; and Noni to eight practically perfect grandchildren. She loves to write, teach and encourage others. Sheri firmly believes the world is looking for faces that have weathered life and still have a smile.

Assigned By Design

Janice Davis

As my husband and I looked at the photos my daughter Randa sent from Hailey's eighth grade dance, we could hardly believe this was the same cherubic five-year-old with a difficult past, but who had now grown into a beautiful and confident teenager.

This had not always been the case with Hailey. She and her younger siblings, Destiny and Tristin experienced various forms of abuse; truly, much more than any child should have to withstand.

As God would have it, ten years ago my daughter had fallen in love with Brett, who was doing everything within his power to keep his children together and to ensure they were safe, fed and had a roof over their head. His three children have two separate mothers, who each struggled with similar but different challenges. As is usually the case, the children suffered the most.

Hailey suffered in silence for years, while her biological mother's live-in boyfriend abused her. Destiny and Tristin struggled with a mommy that was not emotionally healthy, addicted, and unable to provide emotional, physical, or spiritual care.

Randa and Brett married after a brief courtship and suddenly my daughter was no longer a single successful professional. By choice, she was suddenly a bonus caregiver to three children to include a five year old, a three year old, along with an eighteen-month old baby.

Randa laid down her career, travels, and freedom as she surrendered financial security, professional goals, and personal friendships — in essence forsaking everything familiar, in order to begin a path that would be the most difficult and yet the most meaningful mission she had ever endeavored.

Countless school meetings, court dates, clinical psychologist, family therapist, and doctor appointments, quickly became the new normal for Randa. She spent months working on behalf of the oldest child to ensure her predator would not have the opportunity to harm another child.

Standing on the Lord's words enabled Randa and Brett to walk through the very darkest of times. His word helped them to recognize that He has a grand plan for each member of the family. It was a plan that was conceived in their mothers' womb, but with a future designed by God.

The abandonment and abuse each of the children suffered has manifested in a variety of manners to include depression, anxiety, and low self-esteem. Their little hearts struggle to heal and their young minds find it difficult to understand that they had nothing to do with their biological mothers leaving. Yet, when we gather as a family for Sunday dinners, weekend getaways, or holiday celebrations, Tristin brings down the house with his beautiful smile, incredible manners, and heartfelt prayers that would make even Billy Graham proud.

Destiny, the middle child, is a beautiful and bright young lady through and through. The drawings, poems, and music she produces are the envy of many. Hailey's artwork is remarkable. She has an incredible gift of discernment and intellect along with a sunny disposition and a gracious manner that enables her to easily adapt to any situation.

As for my daughter and her husband, marriage is especially challenging yet Randa chose to begin a committed life with a husband and three little ones. During the past decade, my daughter and her husband have spent countless hours in family and marriage therapy, often including the children. The marriage has been incredibly difficult and, yet, they manage to survive and even thrive in spite of the crippling daily challenges.

Although the past decade has been fraught with incredible uphill battles, the family has remained strong in their faith. The payoff for the kids is freedom from fear and neglect, and gratefully each now has two parents that love and nurture them in a healthy manner.

In life there are people the Lord delivers through us and there is family assigned to us. I am so very thankful the Lord chose my daughter to pour love, hope, and a promise for a safe day and a better tomorrow into these wonderful children. A life of faith a freedom.

Janice Ayers Davis is vice-president of an industrial equipment company. Her faith, family, and career are her passion and her ministry. After being challenged in grammar school to write a story using only a random group of words, she was immediately hooked on the pleasure of wrapping a complete story around a single thought.

"Faith is walking face-first and full-speed into the dark. If we truly knew all the answers in advance as to the meaning of life and the nature of God and the destiny of our souls, our belief would not be a leap of faith and it would not be a courageous act of humanity; it would just be...a prudent insurance policy."

— Elizabeth Gilbert

Set Free

Gia L. Wood

When as a prisoner
beaten down
I lay upon the floor.

Tear stained face
ankles chained
staring at the door.

The room is dark
the floor is cold
there's not a single sound.

My stomach aches
my tongue cries out
not a morsel can be found.

I squint my eyes
I scan the dark
looking for the light

I hang my head
defeat sets in
I'm swallowed by the night.

I hear the keys
the door creaks wide
causing my heart to skip a beat.

I hear his steps
I hide my face
afraid our eyes will meet.

The jailer comes
he laughs at me
hatred in his eyes.

I crawl away
ashamed again
I traded truth for lies.

Walking by
he taps the bars
then turns and looks at me.

With laughs and taunts
he cuts my soul
and tells me I'm not free.

He whispers low
between the bars
hateful words of death.

I hide my face
I begin to weep
I scarce can take a breath.

Then he starts
he turns around
fear upon his face.

Light streams in
a man appears
He starts to plead my case.

The jailer hisses -
he says I'm his -
he won me fair and square.

An upheld hand
the jailer stops
there is power in the air!

I lift my head
I lift my eyes
to look Him in the face.

He smiles at me
as if I'm known
the room is filled with grace!

He sees my heart
He knows my thoughts
Though I don't understand.

He lifts His Hands
He shows the scars
"you are engraved upon my hands."

I see his hands
I see his feet
the scars are newly healed.

The death He died
The blood he spilled
My case had been appealed.

He looks at me
with eyes of love
My cell door opens wide.

My chains fall off
He takes my hand
"You're the one for whom I died!"

Gia Wood founded giawoodministries to remind women who they are in Christ. She resides in Central Ohio with her three sons, two sisters, and three dogs! She earned an English degree from Cedarville University. She has a passion for writing in all forms and for speaking the truth of God.

can't
can't
can'
can

A Moment of Failure

Sarah Raines

Freedom exists in the weirdest places and can become real at the oddest times. When we seek it out, realize it, and choose to grasp it, that moment can be life changing.

Last spring, Good Friday in fact, I had a moment of failure. I was at a local pharmacy awaiting my turn for over-the-counter allergy medicine. My ailing, dramatic, 15-year-old daughter was waiting in the car "dying" while I stood in line to ease at least one of her problems. As I waited, I casually looked around the store wondering who might entertain me.

There was a young gal in front of me; she was cute, wearing workout clothes. She was likely coming from or going to the gym. The woman at the counter was oblivious to the line forming behind her. *Ugh*, I thought sarcastically, *yes, please ask another question!* Seconds later, my head whipped to the left. I am certain my mouth was gaping as I heard the awful, angry, and incredibly vulgar words of an absolute train wreck of a woman. She was mad at everyone and everything in her path, including the three little kids with her. She was loud, rude, abrasive, and downright hateful. The worst part was the three kids; they were receiving the brunt of her anger. I was genuinely concerned and the look of disgust on my face was obvious. I hoped against hope she was leaving and taking all of her noisy drama with her. I watched as she weaved through the aisles, shouting along the way. I followed the sound of her screeching and, wouldn't you know it, she landed right behind me. Oh, joy! *Front row seats to this train wreck*, I thought, not quite the entertainment I had in mind.

Long-winded question lady was gone, now it was the cute gal's turn. So close, I could not wait to get my meds and get out. Train wreck mom was turning up the volume, her fury soaring. That's when I heard it, clear as day, "Let her go in front of you." I scoffed at the nudge, quite certain I responded aloud, *"Yeah right."* But seconds later, again in my spirit I heard, "Let her go in front of you…" Ugh, I was annoyed. I justified my response this time… *I'll be two seconds, I'm getting my meds and I'll be gone in a flash.* However, my justification was not sufficient to silence the prompt. "Let her go in front of you!" It was a distinct command that I sharply disobeyed. It was now my turn. As I suspected, I was finished in less than a minute and ready to head to my cranky teenager awaiting relief.

As I started to leave, train wreck moved up and her screaming immediately shifted to the clerk ready to help her. Her anger was seething like venom; my guilt smacked me like a 2x4. I had barely taken a step from the counter and I knew, without question, I had failed. I was not obedient to the prompting of the Holy Spirit. I had an opportunity to be kind to someone who did not deserve it. I had a chance to show love and grace to a mom who, quite possibly, had never experienced this from anyone, ever. I could have shown her the love of Christ in one simple act of kindness. I could have listened to the prompting of the Holy Spirit to "let her go in front of me." I should have listened. I did not.

I went through the remainder of my day with a prick on my heart that I had failed. It grew as I entered into the Good Friday service at church. It pierced me as I thought about how Christ died for this exact sin. On Good Friday, of all days, I could have shown her love. I was so disgusted with myself. Moreover, I could not seek her out even if I wanted to. I never once looked at her face; I was far too busy judging her behavior.

As I sat at that service, I continued to beat myself up. *Now what?* I thought. I cannot go to her. I can't apologize. I can't make it right. I can't fix it. I failed. Period. But what do I do with it? Do I accept defeat? Do I quit trying? Am I forever guilty? I could hear the cutting words of the enemy, "Stop trying, you're a failure!" I could picture the smugness on his wicked face. I had failed, yes. Nevertheless, Jesus died for that failure, for that sin. He paid the price for it. I knew this. Therefore, I had a choice to either remain in bondage or be free. It was that simple. I chose freedom. Immediately my soul lightened as I asked God to forgive me. I will never know the outcome of that woman's fate. I know God will not hold my failure against her.

Later, as I was journaling, I had another realization. Was this failure my opportunity? Was my understanding freedom from failure a lesson all its own? Never does the enemy want us to learn from our mistakes, but instead he wants us to wallow in them. Failure keeps us in bondage, and there is no bondage in Christ. EVER! Therefore, my moment of failure, of shear disobedience, led to an opportunity to accept God's forgiveness and move forward in freedom and confidence.

A simple trip to the pharmacy I will remember forever. A woman I never knew, I will never forget. A freedom I might have never experienced I found in an act of disobedience.

Be open to what God has for you, even in failure. He is bigger than any failure. His love is greater. His grace, unmatched. His forgiveness, unending. Reach out to Him today, right now. Hand over your failure, guilt, and fear; whatever is keeping you in bondage. Let it go, give it up to Jesus. He will take it. He will forgive you. Then you too will experience the amazing, wonderful gift of freedom in Christ.

I'm Sarah Raines. Surrendered follower of Christ. Mother of two teens, two dogs, and two cats. I live and work fulltime in Valparaiso, IN. I seek daily to follow Christ, to be obedient to Him and live in love, freedom, forgiveness, and grace.

Serenade My Soul With Wonder

W. Ruth Esau

Let us acknowledge the Lord, let us press on to acknowledge Him. As surely as the sun rises, he will appear; he will come to us like the winter rains; like the spring rains that water the earth. Hosea 6:3

God's presence is as close as our very breath. This acknowledging of His presence sets our souls free to be all that He created us to be.

> From Peter Pan by JM Barrie

Wendy sighed, to fly! Just think of it! Free of every hindrance and encumbrance!
Soaring, banking swooping! . . .Heavenly was the word that came to mind. . .
. . .Peter laughed again. . .Didn't you know? Faith and trust - that's all it takes—and a pinch of fairy dust!"

C S Lewis similarly felt the modernist's world had neutered the longing, even blurring our perception of God and the spiritual. He also felt Christianity itself had given up the power of pixie dust found in our heart's pursuit of wholeness in order to appear legitimate to the world of modernity—a world built on dry reason and empiricism alone.

Baal-worship sacrificed children, yet God-worship honors children and causes us to see that the hearts and minds of children are what He looks for when He challenges us to become like little children to enter the Kingdom of Heaven. A mind of wonder, of curiosity, a mind free from judgment and negativity. A mind capable of believing.

Reality paralyses us in the " what if's." It keeps us from the freedom that is as close as our breath.

Wonder sets us free to fly through and above the discord, the disappointment, and the pain, and once again allows us to feel the awe of God who is worthy of our faith and trust.

God shows up all over our world but so often we are blinded by the "what if's," so that we don't see Him, and, yet, His breath is so close we realize it only after He passes by.

Would you recognize God if He showed up today?

Where have you stopped long enough to see God is as close as your very breath?

What is making your eyelids heavy and keeping you from seeing the wonder of God's presence in this day?

What might you do to see more fully?

Oh to live in the freedom of the grace and wonder of God's redeeming love.

Serenade My Soul

Lord, meet me in the chaos of my day,

Cause me to know your heart when I feel overwhelmed in the midst of my way.

Speak in softest tones that draw my heart to you.

Serenade my soul, Lord, as I lean into You.

Quiet the restless urgings and anxious thoughts within.
Draw my mind and heart to rest, quieting the chaotic din.
Sing a song of hope and joy that comes from you alone.
Serenade my soul, Lord, I am coming home.

Even as my day is sweet and cares seem so far away.
Keep me focused on You, Lord and all you have to say.
Let my mouth speak forth your praise.
Serenade my soul, Lord as I follow in your ways.

Ruth is an outcome-focused facilitator and coach, inspiring transformative living and leadership. Her own training and development is in executive coaching, emotional intelligence, strengths development, and educational excellence.

Ruth desires to see that those she influences will increase in their personal and professional confidence and competence.

"When you are in troubled and worried and sick at heart
And your plans are upset and your world falls apart,
Remember God's ready and waiting to share
The burden you find much too heavy to bear--
So with faith, "Let Go and Let GOD" lead your way
Into a brighter and less troubled day"

— Helen Steiner Rice

Let Your Daughters Live

Alissa Joy Sande

As I read the final results for the elementary school exams, I felt overwhelming joy and thankfulness. Shakira, my sixteen year old spiritual daughter from Uganda, passed and would be permitted to attend high school. Celebrating this achievement in her life triggered vivid memories of the desperate, three-day battle I waged four years ago for her physical and spiritual freedom. Fighting for this orphan's freedom also commemorated a landmark in my own journey for emotional and spiritual freedom.

Five years before, I'd come to Uganda as a missionary at the age of twenty-nine. I'd waited twenty-two years to fulfill my childhood dream of rescuing the children of Africa. Between childhood and adulthood, much happened to deter me from my divine destiny. Two years prior to moving to Africa, I was divorced, disillusioned, ashamed, and insecure. I felt I'd ruined God's plan for my life and would never become a missionary. One day, as I was searching on the Internet for the least painful way to commit suicide, I felt God say, "If you die, many children in Africa will die." That day was the beginning of cultivating the faith that would propel me to step into my glorious destiny in Christ.

My deepest desire, even more than being a missionary, was to fully surrender my life to God. After I felt the Spirit compelling me, I knew it was time to bring life, joy, and love to the children of Africa. Soon I began a new life in Kyenjojo, Uganda. Not long thereafter, my Ugandan husband and I started a child sponsorship program, medical facility, and elementary school.

Shakira entered our sponsorship program after her father had attempted suicide. She was large in stature and had a natural flare about her. She was full of passion, humor, and spunk; however, you never wanted to be on her bad side. She could box you to the moon in an instant, and her words could shatter you into a million pieces. She was raised by a quarrelsome mother, who was both verbally and physically abusive. Shakira attended our school for one year before the dreadful day that forever defined history for our school, and for Shakira.

That day, our school fellowship began as usual with singing and dancing. When it came time for the preaching, the principal continued to lead the children in a prolonged time of worship. At this moment, hell literally broke loose. More than eight children demonstrated strange behaviors: thrashing their arms and legs, barking like dogs, slithering like snakes, and attempting to bite themselves and others. Teachers and children moved quickly to try to restrain them and pray for them. After receiving prayer, some of the children returned to their normal state. Yet, at least six children continued to manifest demonic behaviors. We decided to take Shakira and the others to the church for more intense prayer.

We squeezed all of the children into the backseat of my Rav4 and drove to church. After about four hours, all of the children normalized except Shakira. She actually became worse. She no longer sounded like herself, and her eyes changed. They were dark and evil and stared coldly into the distance. A voice said, "Shakira is not here. She is gone, but she will die in three days".

A team of teachers, an American intern, and I continued to pray until late in the evening, but the situation remained the same. Shakira used one of her feet as a paintbrush to quickly draw a casket on the floor. She also tried to find anything she could use to tie around her neck or around the beams of the church so she could hang herself. I felt utterly desperate to set this girl free. I continued to pray and decided to fast until she was free.

That first night I slept beside her on the cold, dirty cement floor of our church. I spent the entire night praying for Shakira, rebuking demons, worshipping and praising God in song, and reading the Bible. Every time I began to read the Bible, Shakira curled up with the blanket over her head or plugged her ears and shook her head vigorously back and forth. I dozed off for a few hours only to wake up and begin the whole routine again. As I watched Shakira bound by this unseen force, it became vividly clear to me I was no different than her. I, too, was bound by many unseen forces—fear, guilt, shame, and rejection. These unseen forces held me back from serving the Lord in total freedom, faith, and abandonment. In that moment, I became profoundly aware that instead of being in a position to free others; I was in a position of needing freedom myself. For about an hour, I cried out and prayed for my personal freedom. I prayed the exact scriptures I had prayed for Shakira, except this time I directed them to myself. As I prayed and worshipped, I sensed healing taking place in my own heart and felt shackles being removed from my mind and spirit. After I concluded praying for myself, I directed my attention back to Shakira. Her mental state was unchanged, and she refused to eat or drink anything I offered her.

Over the next twenty-four hours, the American intern and I remained at the church praying for her. We discovered her uncle, a witch doctor, had removed some of her hair and blood to sacrifice her to the dark world, so he could become rich. At various times, Shakira called out his name and then bolted across the room, or tried to jump out the window.

Finally, after the third day, I was extremely desperate. I felt such deep compassion and zealous love for Shakira. I just wanted to see her completely delivered. I thought, *"God, I would do anything to see this girl free!"* In that instant, I heard God say, "I felt the same way, and that is why I sent my Son to die. It was for her freedom and yours." I began to fully direct my eyes to Jesus. I felt a deep, heartfelt gratitude for the price He paid for our freedom. In that moment, God entrusted me with more of His heart and Spirit to equip me to courageously fight for the liberation of Shakira and the many other children who would come after her. The power of the cross was no longer a story in my mind, but a reality deep inside my heart.

Shortly after that exchange, I sensed I was supposed to lie on top of Shakira and breathe life into her. I put my mouth on hers and breathed out deeply a number of times. Each time I breathed into her, she would cry out in a loud, horrific voice. This continued for about five minutes. Then Shakira relaxed and became completely normal. We danced for sheer joy and sang at the top of our lungs in celebration.

Shakira never had another episode after that glorious day. That day also marked a victory flag in my own quest for personal freedom. Witnessing the redemptive work of the cross liberate Shakira enabled me to wholeheartedly believe in its power. Jesus truly paid it all, and all to Him I owe. As I watch both Shakira and I grow into competent, confident young ladies—pursuing our divine destinies, I attribute all glory and praise to Him.

Alissa Joy Sande, a missionary to Africa for nine years, is the founder of Heart for Uganda. This organization releases hope and freedom to children and ministers Christ's love to the lost and destitute. She has a Master's Degree in Literacy, is married with three children, and loves God passionately.

Goodbye Food, Hello Jesus!

Dana Remisovsky

Would I ever be free from this emotional eating that had kept me in bondage for decades? Everything I ever tried, failed. With each attempt to be free, I was defeated by a faceless enemy. I began to believe this was a foe I would never conquer, and one I would be chained to for the rest of my life. That is, until several months ago.

After being a Christian for almost thirty years, I finally decided to consistently spend time with God and read His Word every day. As dramatic as it may sound, this decision has changed my life in such a powerful way. Hebrews 4:12 states, "For the word of God is living and powerful, and sharper than any two-edged sword, piercing even to the division of soul and spirit, and of joints and marrow, and is a discerner of the thoughts and intents of the heart." And Jesus said in John 15:5, "I am the Vine, you are the branches. He who abides in Me, and I in him, bears much fruit; for without Me you can do nothing." These two scriptures are the cornerstones of my experience.

As I abide with God and read His Word daily, I experience a stability in my life I've never had before. Now there is such a buoyancy in my spiritual and emotional life. Prior to making daily time with God my top priority, I experienced chronic depression—for over thirty years. Countless suicidal thoughts were the norm for me. I was on numerous anti-depressant medications and, for a short period of time, was cutting myself. Plus, my relationship with God was a constant rollercoaster. I bounced between love, hate, resentment, anger, and a strong belief that God was withholding from me.

As for the emotional eating, it began when our family moved to another state when I was eight years old. The move meant leaving behind my family, friends, school, and security. This traumatic event pushed me into the welcoming arms of food. I believe the behavior originated when I was a baby and was fed to stop my crying, because in my mind eating equaled comfort. As I grew older, going to food for help came naturally. It was not something I consciously decided to do.

I tried numerous weight loss programs, fad diets, meal replacements, support groups, diet pills, and exercise programs over the years with no long-lasting success. Hopelessness settled in my heart after each failure, and finally I quit trying. Why try when it only results in one failure after another?

Yet, since I have chosen to go to God for comfort, help, and friendship, my dysfunctional relationship with food has come to an end. I can't pinpoint the exact day it happened, but essentially, we broke up. Praise God! Decades of unsuccessfully struggling to break free from this addiction has met its demise. Thank you, Jesus.

I know beyond a doubt there is true freedom in Christ. This freedom didn't cost us anything, but it cost Him everything. Jesus Christ paid the ultimate price for our freedom by sacrificing His life on the cross. We can be set free from sin, fear, anxiety, depression, sickness, and yes, addictions. You may have heard the saying, "I've got you covered." Anything you have been fighting is covered under the blood of Jesus. He's already won the fight. Jesus has done the "heavy lifting," if you will. You don't have to be concerned with trying to "make it happen." He has already made provision for your deliverance. This priceless gift was given to us out of His precious love for us.

Please be encouraged that there is always hope. I've heard hope defined as a confident expectation of good. So, never give up. Honestly, the only way that we are truly hopeless is if we choose to give up. If you have struggled with something for years, or as in my case decades, I implore you to look up.

You may feel powerless compared to something you're struggling with, but God is all-powerful (Ephesians 1:19). You may feel like you've already been defeated, but you have the victory through Jesus Christ (1 Corinthians 15:57). You may feel overcome by a problem, but you are an overcomer (1 John 5:4). You may feel that your battle is impossible to conquer, but with God all things are possible (Matthew 19:26). You are more than a conqueror through Him who loves you (Romans 8:37). Faith and freedom go hand in hand. I experienced freedom when I chose to cultivate my relationship with God. The quality time and attention I have invested has strengthened my relationship with God and drawn us much closer together. I refuse to get back on that spiritual (and emotional) rollercoaster I had been riding for years.

God liberated me from decades of depression and emotional eating, both of which had me not wanting to continue living. That's so foreign to me now. I love life and have so much peace and joy. All the glory goes to God. I want to leave you with Psalm 42:11 as an encouragement, "Why, my soul, are you downcast? Why so disturbed within me? Put your hope in God, for I will yet praise him, my Savior and my God."

Dana is an encourager who is relentless about fulfilling God's plan for her life. She is new to writing, which God placed on her heart to do just over one year ago. Her desire is to uplift, bring hope, and point others to Christ through her writing and in her personal life. Check out her "Devotions with Dana" Facebook, Twitter, and Instagram accounts as well as her website devotionswithdana.com.

faith

SUBSTANCE OF THINGS HOPED FOR

evidence OF THINGS NOT SEEN

Only Faith in Jesus Spells Freedom

Robert Harmon

How can faith and freedom come together in American society? We all know of the battles this country has fought to preserve our freedoms. As for faith, well, we have more faiths and non-faiths than probably any country on earth. As Americans, we pride ourselves on how we accept everyone—tolerance is our new religion. It is this acceptance of everything that has become one of the biggest challenges we face in America.

Many of our fellow Americans are so consumed with chasing freedom in every aspect of their lives, they don't realize there is only one answer for human freedom—and His name is Jesus. Jesus said, "And ye shall know the truth, and the truth shall make you free" (John 8:32, KJV). Only through faith and turning your life over to the One who created life, can freedom be found. So how does this apply to the America of today?

The Biblical "basics of faith" in American public life, are being erased by those who believe freedom means a furthering of the separation between "church and state." Certain lawyers and judges have, in past years, been able to minimize or eradicate the Ten Commandments in many public places. Other religions, or non-religions, have been able to get people interested in joining their causes by either suppressing Jesus and the church or, by equivocating their "gods" to Jesus.

So where are the Christians and what are they doing? Many of those who call themselves Christians look and act just like any other "freedom-loving" American. If non-Christians can see no difference in being Christian, why should they change?

And what about you? Are you the kind of "freedom-loving" American who only makes time for human-based activities, or do you also make time for God? When my only children, twin girls, moved away and started college a couple of years ago, I found it very hard to endure their absence. I quickly gave up my ritual of "reading the newspaper" every morning, and instead I read from the Bible until the coffee finished brewing and it was time for breakfast. Sometimes I read the Bible before bedtime, especially after a long road trip, as a thanks to God for safe travel. As a result, I have now read through the entire Bible and have begun a second reading—something I should have done years ago.

This Bible-reading has had other unexpected consequences. I find I am praying more than "just at bedtime." My activities involve more "God-centered" activities than before. In addition to acting in short Christian films, I am now writing Christian entertainment. I have been working on two screenplays and plan to finish a novel started over a decade ago. Through reading the Bible and doing Christian activities, I feel more freedom from sin and unfruitful activities. Being a Christian involves more than just praying and attending church on Sunday; it means much Bible reading and acting on what God wants you to do. Nothing is more satisfying in life than experiencing God's peace by being where He wants you to be.

If you are one of those Christians who is too busy to find time for God, what are you showing others about the values in your life? Most of us have to work for a living. But what of your free time? Take a hard look at where you spend your free time. For example, if you spend more time watching television or attending sporting events than reading the

Bible or doing Christian activities, does this reflect a faith in God and His freedom or man and his freedom? Only through a continual faith in God is real freedom found. And the only God of anyone's life should be Jesus. Jesus said, "I am the way, the truth, and the life: no man cometh unto the Father, but by me" (John 14:6 KJV). Freedom as a Christian does not mean you are free to do whatever you want. Once you are saved, your life should be spent in a pursuit of holiness or becoming more like Jesus.

There was a song I memorized and sang when I was in first grade. The first line of the song went, "God bless America, land that I love." God will bless America if Christians continue to share our faith in God, and the freedom of a life lived correctly and victoriously through Him. A fitness center instructor friend of mine says, "The root problems of the human body go to having a strong core." The Bible states how Jesus should be at our core. "I am the vine, ye are the branches: He that abideth in me, and I in him, the same bringeth forth much fruit: for without me ye can do nothing" (John 15:5 KJV).

My sincere desire would be for everyone to have such a strong faith in Jesus so we could become a beacon of hope to show others the way to true freedom in Him. "Let your light so shine before men, that they may see your good works, and glorify your Father which is in heaven" (Matthew 5:16 KJV). Let us be worthy of our faith and our calling, to share Christ's freedom to a needy nation and world. And let us never forget, the only way to experience real freedom is through a continual faith in our Lord and Savior, Jesus Christ.

Robert Harmon is an Oklahoma Petroleum Geologist with a desire to be involved in Christian entertainment. His spare time is spent writing a novel and screenplays - while performing in Christian short films. He and his wife, Angela, are parents to twin girls and reside in Owasso, Oklahoma.

Forgiven and Free

Deedy Tripp

"I don't care if they die. It wouldn't bother me at all. I doubt I'd shed a single tear."

My sister, Cathy, and I sat on the front steps of her house talking about our parents. I was seething with hatred for both of them. Cathy had been instrumental in my coming to Christ and was a mentor to me in my new walk with Jesus. When questions about scripture came up, it was to her that I turned. I had been a Christian for only a short time and was learning so much about what that meant. I wanted to learn all I could about God and His word — I was starving for it. He had saved me from completely destroying my life and the lives of my boys with drugs, alcohol, and promiscuity. It was only by God's grace that I was alive.

"You're going to have to forgive them, Deedy," she said quietly.

"No, I don't! I will hate them until the day I die!" I spewed back. "They don't deserve my forgiveness!"

You see, my stepfather had molested me from the time I was eight years old until my suicide attempt at the age of thirteen. When I blurted out what he had done to me during a heated family argument a few years later, nothing happened. Nothing! He left as usual after the big fights, and my mom ran off to her bedroom, slamming the door behind her. That was it. No questions. No comments. Nothing!

The next day, having remembered his threats to me when I was little, I was scared. When my mother got home from work, I told her that I was moving out, that I didn't want to make her choose between me and my stepfather. She told me she had no intention of choosing between us, and she would not allow me to move out. I threatened to file charges against him with the police. Shocked and unwilling to have our "dirty laundry" aired in public, she relented and allowed me to move in with my oldest sister.

But the words she'd spoken felt like a slap in the face and a knife in my heart, "I have no intention of choosing between you." It was the ultimate rejection. My own mother refused to come to my rescue or even try to defend me.

Over the years, a deep-seated hatred and resentment took hold of my heart. On the outside, I was happy-go-lucky, but on the inside I was searching for love and acceptance. I needed to be wanted and began my search with drugs, alcohol, partying, and promiscuity.

"Deedy, do you think you deserved for Jesus to forgive you?" Cathy's question brought me back to the present. Growing up I had despised that sweet little voice she used in framing her question. But now it was just plain unsettling.

I jumped up, ready to end the conversation. "I never did the things that he did! I would never have chosen *him* over my own kids, like she did!"

I went home but couldn't get her words out of my mind. While reading my Bible, they would play back, over and over. . . "do you think you deserved Jesus' forgiveness?" Then I came across the passage where Jesus said, "If you don't forgive others, your Father in heaven won't forgive you." Ouch!

I kept reading, deciding that it wasn't talking about *my* situation. Surely, Jesus didn't expect me to forgive *them*. Just look at all that had happened over the years. No. I didn't have to forgive them.

So, I kept reading. But it wouldn't go away.

A couple days later, I was reading about the crucifixion. Tears were streaming down my face as I read about all the suffering that Jesus had endured for me. Then I came to the passage, just before He died, where He said, "Father, forgive them, for they know not what they do."

I fell on my knees, sobbing. I didn't deserve such a great sacrifice! How could He forgive them? How could He forgive me?!!

"Oh God, I know I have to forgive, but I don't know how! You've forgiven me for so much. I know I would be dead if it were not for You. But if You want me to forgive them, You're going to have to make it happen. I CHOOSE to forgive, Father. You have to make me *feel* it."

Every day I said that prayer. Every day I chose to forgive. It wasn't a feeling. It was a choice. But eventually, as the days, weeks, months, and even a few years went by, I realized I had forgiven. I no longer hated them. After several years, I realized I had even grown to love them. That doesn't mean I allowed my kids to be at risk—I didn't. Forgiveness doesn't mean forgetfulness. But I forgave and became very involved in their care in their later years in life.

One day, when my stepfather was facing a serious life-threatening surgery, I sat down at their kitchen table and shared my testimony with my stepfather. I told him how I had been involved with drugs and partying, and how Jesus had worked in many ways to draw me to Himself. I told him how I accepted God's salvation and all the ways He had changed me since. I led my stepfather in a prayer to receive Jesus as his Savior that night.

Forgiveness. When I chose to forgive, Jesus made it happen. But that forgiveness wasn't as much for my parents as it was for me. Jesus promised not only to forgive me when I came to Him, He promised to set me free. And He did. Forgiveness toward them equaled freedom for me.

"You shall know the truth, and the truth shall set you free. . . So, if the Son makes you free, you will be free indeed." (John 8:32, 36 NIV)

I've found freedom through faith in Jesus. Have you?

Deedy Tripp is married to her best friend Mike Tripp. They live in Frostproof, Florida, where she is a construction business owner, a goat farmer, and a conference speaker and Bible teacher. She enjoys spending time with her two sons and daughters-in-law, but especially with their five grandchildren.

She Loves Jesus and America Too

Jenny Maass Klobuchar

Silence hung over the dusty book layers of the outdated library. Dark panicking eyes darted around the room. There it was again. It was unmistakable this time. The doorknob, jerked and jarring, rattled loudly by the insistent intruder locked outside the underground church meeting.
My heart raced, beating out of my chest. "Was today the day we would be caught?" I was paralyzed with fear.

"Oreos and Coke!" one quiet but urgent voice of broken English commanded from the meeting circle. The attendees immediately responded to these mysterious code words. Bang, bang, bang! The door rattled loudly, heightening anticipation. Bibles, visible all around the circle of guests, quickly disappeared under chairs or bottoms. Communication had dwindled to quiet nods and small shuffling. Suddenly, plastic packaging nudged my arm and snapped me out of a fearful trance. "Please, take Oreo," the voice offered. I looked up to realize our secret Bible study had transformed into a very casual circle of an English conversation party, calmly sharing Coke and Oreos. I smiled and knowingly joined the charade.

A final desperate fist-pound rang out again at the door. Bang! Bang! Bang! We watched as the designated student approached and slowly began to unlock the door. This was it. The future of these believers' rest in the identity of the unknown intruder. How did they find us? What gave away our location? Like a slow-motion horror movie the door creaked its way wide revealing the dark silhouette of native

Chinese. My heart dropped into my stomach. The painful moment hung for an eternity. Suddenly the room burst into unintelligible sounds. Voices and breath released all around me, swelling in the room in a confusing jumble. What should I do? Run? Hide? Cry. . .fight?

The intruder pushed past the door and hurried in straight toward our circle. Students all over the room jumped up; chair metal scuffling on bare concrete floors and Mandarin voices speaking out all at once. It was an onslaught of noise. I was frozen—lost, confused, and scared. A half-bitten Oreo hung limply in my hand. Then I looked up, horrified.

"We want to kill you!" one student screamed as he reached out grabbing the intruder in an embrace. Hysteria swelled around the two until suddenly the whole room broke into laughter. Students began hugging and exchanging relieved smiles. With a big grin he repeated, "We want to kill you, you make us so nervous!" he yelled at his classmate in broken English. Sweet release flooded my soul. With a deep breath I relaxed my nerves and embraced the scene, taking it all in. That day changed my life. Never again would I take any Bible study meeting so lightly. I felt as if I had survived a secret church initiation.

Some months later, our underground church meeting concluded from a different location. I exited the tiny apartment of the fourth floor and was happy to see the Chinese believers dispersing into adjoining rooms for additional prayer and fellowship. Our songs of worship, though whispered quietly behind closed doors, still rang loudly in my head. I grabbed my guitar and headed for the hallway. I felt so exhilarated and free. Our Christian faith had been safely and joyfully celebrated in a closed Communist country. Like trying to keep a lit flashlight undetected in a dark room, my face glowed with streams of light from our Savior. I decided to channel my joy into a popular American song, Tom Petty's "Free Falling." I began to hum along quietly, stroking the familiar chords.

Then faintly in the background, joining my concert of one, was the tinkle of percussion. A steady sound of jingling keys was rising up the stairwell. I calmly peered over the banister and recognized the uniformed arm of a Communist Party Official. He was sliding his hand up the rail and racing up the stairs toward me! With a quick glance over my shoulder, I could see our assembly had all but disappeared and the room doors were shut. "You're too late for them," I thought with a big grin, happy that the faith and fate of my Chinese friends were free from harm's way. I merrily played along counting the flights as he continued climbing. Though danger was closing in, I sang out quietly "and I'm free…free falling."

The sweaty brow of the dark man appeared on the landing, spotted me, and rushed the final steps up to my floor. Now I hummed along with pronounced strums. He looked at me, then looked down the empty hallway. The floor was deserted. I could see the frustration in his eyes. I smiled politely and kept playing, relaxed against the railing. With fury on his face he flashed a look of warning my way and then stubbornly marched back down the stairs. I smiled broadly and carried on, "She loves Jesus…and America too."

Jenny Maass Klobuchar began the college ministry, *EighteenTwentyThree*, at Harborside Christian Church. She founded this movement to reach millennials and unchurched of the next generation. Jenny speaks truth by giving "the real deal," challenging youth and adults alike to rise up as followers of Christ and live out the truth in their lives. Learn about Jenny's speaking and writing ministry at www.jennymaass.com

"We hold these truths to be self-evident: that all men are created equal; that they are endowed by their Creator with certain unalienable rights; that among these are life, liberty, and the pursuit of happiness."

Thomas Jefferson

"Freedom is never more than one generation away from extinction. We didn't pass it to our children in the bloodstream. It must be fought for, protected, and handed on for them to do the same."

Ronald Reagan

Set Free

Barbara Riffenburg

"It is for freedom that Christ has set us free. Stand firm, then, and do not let yourselves be burdened again by a yoke of slavery" (Galatians 5:1).

Broken and feeling like you're dying inside… everyday more and more

When will it all come to fruition and hit the floor?

Your world comes crashing down, splattering pieces of you everywhere.

Holding on to the last of your sanity is sometimes more than you can bear.

Screaming out loud for help, thinking you're all alone in this brokenness.

Feeling so raw, every ounce of shame but, then came Jesus!

Jesus, who has the power to break every chain, shackle, and binding you possess

Broken chains through the blood of Christ; now you can finally raise your eyes and be blessed.

Hold your faith and the gift of freedom He has given you

for it's to share in helping others who feel the way you do.

Soon enough your eyes will see what He can do through your willingness to share willingness to share your faith and freedom with other who have similar burdens to bear.

Have you ever felt so broken you would never be put back together? The pain so intense you didn't know how you would get through the day? Did you ever feel so unloved that every bone in your body just ached? Felt shattered and broken wondering what your life would ever amount to? So you ask, where is this faith and freedom?

Ask the Lord to help you get rid of those chains. He listens to your prayers even when you think He's not. All of a sudden your chains and shackles will be gone, because of the one and only Lord Jesus Christ. Cleansed by His blood and able to move about freely again, He has shown me the way to be rid of those shackles forever. Faith is Freedom!

Barbara was born and raised in Goodells, Michigan. She has been married to Dale since August 2008, and between the two of them they have 5 children and 2 grandchildren. She has been a Pharmacy Technician for 24 years. Barbara loves to write poetry and devotions. She has been attending Westminster Church for 16 years and loves doing devotionals for Christmas and Mother's Day. Barbara has been to Costa Rica on two mission trips and loves serving the Lord.

The Freedom of Faith

Destiny Whitfield

I was brought into this world with a bit of a rough beginning. I was born on March 16, 2005 and had at least one loving parent, my Father. My mother was young and my father did everything he could to provide for us. But when I was at the age of four my mother left us. You know how they say 'out with the old and in with the new,' that is what my stepmom is to me, the new. She is my everything. I told her recently that I love her more than I love myself. When I am with her I feel the freedom to be myself. I do not feel like I have to impress anyone. She lead me to Christ and never gave up on me like my mom did.

At my Baptism, when I was lifted out of the water I felt as if I had been made new.

Everyone rose to their feet and started clapping for me. I confess that I didn't know the true meaning of Baptism. It wasn't till much later that I realized I just made the biggest decision of my life. I thought since I devoted my life to Christ through Baptism

I wouldn't have as much freedom. I finally came to a realization that being a Christian

doesn't limit your freedom, it increases your freedom. Now I am totally free to share my

testimony and help others.

My name is Destiny Whitfield and I am 13. I live in Marietta, Georgia with my Father, Step-mother, and my Sister and Brother, and our adorable family dog.

Sweet Freedom

Carol Ensminger

I have a love-hate relationship with food. I love to dip a sweet chocolate and mint Oreo cookie sandwich into a tall glass of milk, savoring every bite. But then, I hate food because it inevitably shows up as extra pounds. Every time I look at the increased number on the scale, I beat myself up. Every. Single. Time.

Like most women, I struggle with body image, love unhealthy foods, and have extra pounds hanging around. So years ago, I began my quest for that "miracle" diet. I tried every diet and diet pill that was available and even tried not eating at all. When those desperate measures didn't get me where I wanted to be, I started to dabble with bulimia for more years than I care to admit. I'm sure you have heard the saying, "Desperate times call for desperate measures." I am grieved over some of the ridiculous things I have done to be skinny.

Although I lost many pounds over the years, they always came back, usually bringing unwanted friends along with them. I blamed everyone and everything—except myself—for my issues with food. I accused the busyness of an active young family, an abusive relationship, or the loss of a loved one. When the slightest life disappointment was thrown my way, the Oreos and milk would be right by my side to comfort me.

During those years, I was on a roller-coaster of unhealthy eating patterns—emotional ups and downs, weight losses and gains. And like most of us, I got way too comfortable with this cycle of failure in my life and didn't want to spend the time and effort changing it. It felt hopeless. As I lay my head down at the end of the day, I'd tell myself there's always tomorrow.

I would often pray for God to remove the cravings and the pounds, yet I didn't wake up skinny with intense cravings for fruit, vegetables, and all the foods containing nutrients my body so desperately needed. I wish I were being melodramatic and exaggerating here, but I'm not.

Paul knew what it felt like to have struggles that wouldn't go away. In 2 Corinthians 12, we read that Paul desperately begged and pleaded to have the thorn in his side removed (vs. 8). But God didn't reach down and instantly pluck out Paul's thorn. Instead, He gave Paul a promise: "My grace is sufficient for you, for my power is made perfect in weakness" (vs. 9). God does not intend us to be weak, but when we are weak, we are made strong through Him.

I tried fat-free, sugar-free, gluten-free, dairy-free, and, sadly, calorie-free. Nothing worked. Then one day I figured out what I was doing wrong—I was also eating Christ-free.

I learned that my problem was more than carrying around a few extra pounds. I had a spiritual problem, and until I remedied that, committing to any health plan would be useless. I discovered that I didn't need to go on a diet; I needed to go on a journey—a spiritual one. A journey that offers freedom, not deprivation. A journey full of grace instead of condemnation.

Here's what I know about desperate situations: they can take us away from God or they can lead us to have greater dependence on Him. He knows our shortcomings and empathizes with our weakness, but we also have to realize that our weaknesses make room for His power. Knowing this truth is the key to liberty and freedom from our bondage, strongholds, and addictions (John 8:32).

I don't know what you struggle with today, but I want you to remember God gives us the same promise today as He gave Paul—He will make us strong when we are weak. Time and time again, I have seen God can't resist those who humbly and honestly admit how desperately they need Him.

No matter how many foolish things I've done, or how many times I have failed, He loves me. The same goes for you. He will still use us in ways that we cannot even begin to imagine. Honestly, I believe He will, and I believe, if you look around, you'll recognize that He is already at work in your life.

I'm not a dietician or a Bible scholar, and I don't have it all figured out. I am absolutely a work in progress in many areas. This is one of them. I still eat things I shouldn't, but now I do so without letting the voice of condemnation speak louder than the voice of freedom. Nothing can keep God's power from me, and nothing can separate me from His love. Nothing. Not even a bag of Oreos.

Carol is a Bible teacher, mentor, and writer whose passion is encouraging women to live healthier lives from the inside out. She loves to help women grow so they can be all that God created them to be. She and her husband live in Arizona and have six children and nine grandchildren.

Lord of All

Linda Coulson

Trust in the Lord with all your heart and lean not on your own understanding; in all your ways submit to him, and he will make your paths straight (Proverbs 3: 5-6).

Trust in the Lord. My heart says God knows what is best for me and I should trust him. But sometimes getting my head to believe my heart is a challenge. To be truthful, I like *my life* to have *my plan*. My plan is well thought out, known in advance, and logical. When life starts moving too far off course and things get a little too uncomfortable, that is when worries start to surface…the what ifs. And what ifs can quickly turn to fear. And fear can overpower faith putting a stop to my trust in God.

I hear of people praying bold prayers like, "Lord I will go where you want me to go and do what you want me to do." But I also know that God takes those bold prayers and sometimes whisks people away to remote places in the world. This possibility is scary. So, instead I pray timid prayers like, "Lord, I come to you and pray for you to use me… within my reason."

That is where our patient and loving God meets me. God uses our timid little "yes" and then grows our feeble trust into a bigger "yes." He shows us there is a freedom in opening our hands and letting go of the control. As we step out in faith, He carries us, and little by little our worries grow smaller. Then our hearts become lighter, we are braver, and we take back the joy that was stolen from us by worry and fear.

When God places something on my heart, I will consider it for a few minutes. I will try to talk myself out of thinking that God placed that idea on my heart. After all, why would He want me to do that? That idea is out of my comfort zone. I don't understand what the outcome could be, so I want to dismiss the idea. Then, my heart will quicken. I will feel excited and nervous all at once, and I will want to push this thought away and bury it down deep. Usually these thoughts are to call, reach out, visit, or write to someone. Sadly, sometimes I don't say "yes." Multiple excuses—of not finding time in my schedule, someone else will do it, or I will get to it eventually—fill my mind and I say "no."

Sometimes I do say "yes." I make the time, leave my comfort zone, and I reach out. I open my hands and feel the blessings. So why do I drag my feet when the Lord calls? He created me and He knows what is best. He knows what I need. His way points to life and joy, but regardless of these truths, sometimes I want to run and hide. God sees us where we are, even when we are hiding. He walks with us, bringing us closer to his heart.

Along this dance of three steps forward and two steps back, God loves to throw in His sense of humor. One day, He placed a whisper on my heart, a whisper of the idea of Africa. I pushed this down deep.

No, I am wife and mother. I am a teacher and a homemaker, not someone who travels to foreign countries for mission work. This was not reasonable or logical and certainly not in my comfort zone. Fear swept over me. What ifs rose up, took control, and tried to bury the whisper. The idea was pushed aside. *I don't need to go to Africa. I am back in control of this part of my life.* But there is nothing pushed down too deep for God. So the whisper on my heart rose again. God met me where I was, held my hand, and my fears. He wanted to show me He hears.

My husband and I ended up saying "yes" and traveled to Uganda, Africa. This was the beginning of our hearts being broken and filled back up with God's love. There we saw orphans, who mean nothing to this world, praising Jesus. They were so thankful and joyful. They gave glory to God for everything in their lives, even though it was nothing by the world's standards. The peace I felt there was so strong. And in a matter of moments, that red dirt on my shoes from a hillside half a world away worked into my heart forever.

So my response now when God whispers, when He challenges my carefully laid plans, is to remember He is the Lord of all. I can trust Him even when I don't understand. I can say "yes," and there is freedom in that word.

Linda Coulson lives in rural Pennsylvania with her husband, two daughters and, God willing, a third daughter on the way from China. She is a homemaker, teacher and an advocate for children everywhere. After visiting Africa with HeartforUganda.org, Linda speaks out for the least of these and God's amazing miracles.

"Faith is the bird that feels the light and sings when the dawn is still dark."

Rabindranath Tagore

"For you were called to freedom, brothers. Only do not use your freedom as an opportunity for the flesh, but through love serve one another."

Galatians 5:13

My Beloved Child

Stacy Robert

So small and so tiny. A little burst of light placed deeply within the heart of the Father. Lovingly, longingly, the Father reaches deep within himself to draw her forth.

"Who will she be?" the angels whisper in reverence to the Almighty.

"She will be my light. She will be my Love. She will draw many back to me," the Father responds. "I am taking her from my heart and I know she shall soon return back to me."

The hope and wonder of it all is so palpable in the room. "Where will she go?" they all whisper once again.

"I have a tree whose roots go back to my tree of life. This is the line. . .so many blessings from those who have gone before. So many opportunities for one such as this," He responds.

"But what of the separation—the breaks in the branches. How will fruit appear with so much to repair?" the angles once again ponder.

"With great compassion and love, also with mystery and sincerity," the Father responds, "Time and my love will heal all wounds. I will take on the separation and mend it myself. Can't you see the roots? The good full roots? This is a tree that has been planted by my living water."

With that He gracefully gestures to a mighty and beautiful river flowing from the very throne He now sits upon.

"But what of the accuser? Look, He is waiting now in the courtyard—ready, waiting. He has a plan as well," they once again respond.

To this the Father lets out a soft chuckle. "Wisdom and grace, I give to this little one. She may take time, but she will overcome every accusation by the words of her testimony and by the blood of the Lamb."

One more response could be heard— "Yes, but her suffering. What of that? Can she withstand the harsh road ahead? The hurt, the pain? Father, the grief–will it be too much?"

To this the Father's face saddens. "My beloved child will endure much. All suffering will not be in vain. For the pain she feels will draw her deeper and closer to the place of her origination than ever before." As He speaks He gestures back to His heart.

Whatever grief has been etched upon His face is now replaced with radiant joy, total victory and love. This love is so rich and amazing it blazes through His eyes like an all-consuming fire.

With that, all the voices are hushed in reverence and awe. Lovingly, He places the light gently into the great and mighty river that flows from His mercy seat of grace, and then whispers the words, "Live. . . ."

At the same moment on earth a mother's womb is opened and new life begins to take form. Nine months later a beautiful baby girl is born. Her earthly name is given, and it means, Resurrected One, or One Who Shall Rise Again. Her parents have no clue they have given their daughter such a prophetic name. Just as in the days of old, the name defines her–although her parents have no clue at the time how it will happen.

She is a curious and wide-eyed baby. With stars in her eyes and music in her heart. She loves her new world. Never knowing or understanding just how long it has been since she left her true home with her heavenly Father to journey to this strange new land.

Stacy Robert is passionate about bringing the words of the Bible to life for every reader no matter their age. She is privileged to be writing and filming curriculum studies over the past two years at a congregation of over 4000 people in Arizona.

"Sorrow looks back, Worry looks around, Faith looks up"

> Ralph Waldo Emerson

"Reason is in fact the path to faith, and faith takes over when reason can say no more."

> Thomas Merton

Breaking Free

Dawn Mann

After our family's Easter gathering, I was making the long drive back home. While speeding along the expressway, suddenly a flashing light flashed in my rearview mirror. As I stood outside my vehicle with the lights from the patrol car blinding my eyes, I felt humiliated. I finally realized I was being arrested when the last click of the handcuffs clicked tightly on my arms behind my back.

One minute I was driving, the next minute I was sitting in the back of a patrol car telling myself, "It was just two drinks!" As I sat there alone and scared on that frightful night in the local county jail, I started to comprehend that all of my means of freedom on this earth were swiftly being locked away. The car had been towed and the license plate removed and cut up into pieces, and now I sat in jail.

Later when the trial was finally over, I realized my conviction. I felt I had "DUI" stamped across my forehead for the world to see. No more license, and sobriety court was my sentence. This was a year of extreme strict court orders; calling in everyday for drug testing, and every week I had to attend at least three recovery meetings, individual therapy, and appointments that alternated between a case manager or the judge. There was no mercy under the court system. You were very careful not to make even the slightest mistake because after two strikes, whether your fault or not, it landed you back in jail to finish your sentence. I was extremely grateful to be granted a restricted license as long as I had a wired blower intact. The license I had only allowed me to drive from point A to point B, which was approved prior to granting me the license. Having the blower installed, meant I had to blow into a mouthpiece before starting my car and periodically it would ask for samples while driving. Even though I was grateful for the precautions that come with the restricted license, I felt isolated and trapped. Not being able to move about freely, I found myself spending much more time alone with Jesus. He brought me comfort and never left my side. An intimate love relationship grew during that shackled, but treasured time. Jesus became my One true source. In the past, when I had longed for peace, I found it momentarily by numbing myself with alcohol, but I was never truly filled with peace. My heart was aching with unbearable pain, but I had no way to cope.

During this time, I allowed God to take His Healing Hand to my inner core as I opened up my heart. I allowed Him to dig up the buried wounds, which were caused from past emotional, sexual, and spiritual abuse. These wounds had also created a fear of men, which led to a confused sexual identity. This newfound relationship with Jesus was now a passion and I wanted Him to be my example for everything.

God kept showing His face and, coupled with a faithful love of others, I took steps of faith out of my comfort zone. It was not easy, but I learned to trust in the Lord who penetrated my heart and soul. The more I got to know Him, the more my heart desired to follow His lead. His Word became my lifeline as it illuminated the darkness and, even though I was no longer locked up physically behind prison doors, I had been living in a darkness that held me captive.

This new freedom in Christ became my safety net against the world of deadly destruction. Jesus rescued me out of the darkness. He came and snapped open the chains that kept me bound. Hearing me cry out in desperation, He cut through the steel bars, and He opened up the gates of freedom. After that dreadful night in jail, I encountered Jesus when my life's choices came to nothing. He pursued me. His love for me was shown by Him never giving up on me, yet allowing me to fall.

I still undergo hardship, but I have found that my faith grows stronger as it is stretched. These are the times I have to dive deeper into Gods Word. I have had to make a conscious choice: *"Will I allow my past to define me as a failure or will I take my experiences and allow God to use it for His Will."*

The life I strive to live every day is directed by a faith in Jesus. I desire not to return to the bondage of slavery and live in that torturous fear, but instead I desire to be led by the Spirit of God. One thing I have learned is that there is no place too dark that the light illuminated by the love of God cannot reach. My heart humbly submits to Him today because He is daily delivering me from tormenting fears that still try to take hold.

Walking in obedience is the new path set before me that gives me peace. Today, I hold onto His teachings and stay committed to His word. The scripture says that when you know the truth, the truth will set you free. In Him and through faith in Him, I found the truth. I may approach God with freedom and confidence. I now choose to live fearlessly by faith and praying (instead of drinking), through all things.

Jesus has redeemed my past and I am now set free to be a prisoner of Christ.

God planted a desire in Dawns heart to be a writer and speaker through His intense work and call on her life to see people who are broken to become free and unashamed in Christ. Dawn Mann passionately loves the Lord and now dedicates her life serving Him.

"Blessed is the nation whose God is the Lord, the people He choose for His inheritance."

Psalm 33:12

"...Religion requires freedom. How then does religion require freedom? Well this is the simplest of all to understand. Today we need only consider the Middle East or, God help them, North Korea. Religion is the most fragile of all freedoms. And that's because it is the most threatening to those in power."

Eric Metaxas

Gifts of Faith from My Heart Tree

Dyann Shepard

"To everything there is a season, and a time to every purpose under the heaven: A time to get, and a time to lose; a time to keep, and a time to cast away" (Ecclesiastes 3:1,6).

When we moved to Atascadero thirty years ago, we had a beautiful oak tree in our front yard. Every morning as I enjoyed my quiet time with the Lord I looked out at my tree. It was tall, strong, and shaded our front yard. I loved my tree and what it provided. Over the years, friends began telling me that the main branch, and the source of shade, was dead and needed to be removed, but I couldn't let it go. One day, a friend came and announced he was cutting off the branch. Afterwards, to my surprise, the tree began to thrive. It looked different, but it had a new beauty. This was the beginning of many lessons of faith and trust from my tree, which continue even today.

There have been many gifts from my tree. There was the obvious one; years of firewood. But there has been a far more important gift. When the branch came down, it revealed a surprise. Something I would have missed if the branch had remained. A huge heart was etched in the trunk where the branch had been. It was a hidden gift. Over the next twenty years, I enjoyed watching the birds fly in and out of the heart on the tree as they sang their morning songs. The heart served as a sweet reminder from the Lord that when I cling too tightly to loved ones, possessions, the past, etc., I may be missing a God-gift.

Jesus said in John 15:2, "Every branch in me that does not bear fruit, He takes away and every branch that bears fruit, He prunes so it may bear more fruit." How often I have clung to my old dry branches. I often resist when I feel the presence of the Lord's pruning shears. I want to hold on to my old branches. I am used to them. They provide emotional shade for me. However, this simple hidden treasure brought opportunities to share with clients and friends the gift of faith that grew from my heart tree. When they asked, "Did you know there is a heart on your tree? Wow, there is a heart on your tree," I was able to share how the Lord stretched my faith as I began to "let go." By letting go of people and things that are precious to me, I have experienced the joy of God's provision in my life and in the lives of those I love.

My children have matured in spiritually deeper ways as I have ceased holding them too tightly. Most recently, my heart tree helped me let go of a ministry I loved when it became apparent my husband wanted to change churches. He didn't ask me to leave but I knew he wasn't happy. I loved our church, the people, and the ministry I was involved with. I didn't want to let go. Privately, I cried and prayed. As I sat in my prayer chair looking out the window at my heart tree, I asked myself, "Was I willing to put what I had learned to the test? *Was I willing to let go and have faith that God had something new for me?*" After much struggle, I asked my husband to choose a new church. I told him, "As long as they love the Lord, I'll be Ok."

There were so many new gifts waiting to be revealed in our new church. My husband was happier, more relaxed, and grew spiritually which was a great joy for me. I began to desire a deeper biblical study, which led me to reach out to friends and clients from various denominations to join me in a spiritual journey using only the Word of God. This has been enormously rewarding. My walk with the Lord has deepened in surprising ways. I don't think this desire would have surfaced if we had remained at our former church, since the teaching was so fulfilling.

I began attending "Sisters of the Heart," a women's fellowship group. It was a new experience in faith for me. After a spiritual topic is presented, each of us finds a quiet spot to meditate, pray, and journal. Later, there is a time of sharing what the Lord revealed to our heart. This meditative, thoughtful, fellowship resulted in fresh growth and freedom in my faith walk with the Lord. It has birthed a deeper peace and trust. I would have missed this sweet blessing of new sisters in the Lord if I had not let go of our prior church.

My tree is gone now, a victim of a drought. One morning, I looked out to my heart tree and realized something was terribly wrong. It had died. Once again, I was crying "No, no, not my tree." It was a symbol of hidden gifts. Always there, faithfully every morning, reminding me to be open to new things, and to be willing to let go. It couldn't be dead. But it was. Now I had to be willing to let go of the very symbol that had taught me to let go.

The morning the tree came down, my friend, Ann, brought me the book "The Giving Tree." I read it through my tears. Fortunately, the Lord provided an excellent craftsman who saved the heart and made a beautiful bench for me.

My tree has been repurposed. My heart tree is now my heart bench. It serves as a reminder that as I walk in faith God always has a purpose. As I now prepare for retirement, I know God will repurpose my life just as He did my tree. What new gifts will I discover? What new growth will sprout in my life?

Dyann Shepard is a wife, mother, grandmother, Certified Public Accountant, and biblical small group facilitator. She loves to share how God can redeem, restore and bless, particularly through life's most tumultuous challenges. Dyann was formerly on staff with CRU, as was a Stephen's Minster for over ten years.

Living Parables of Central Florida

Living Parables of Central Florida, Inc., of which EABooks Publishing is a division, supports Christian charities providing for the needs of their communities and are encouraged to join hands and hearts with like-minded charities to better meet unmet needs in their communities. Annually the Board of Directors chooses the recipients of seed money to facilitate the beginning stages of these charitable activities.

Mission Statement

To empower start up, nonprofit organizations financially, spiritually, and with sound business knowledge to participate successfully as a responsible 501(c)3 organization that contributes to the Kingdom work of God.

Incubator Program

The goal of the Incubator Program: The Small Non-Profit Success Incubator Program, provides a solid foundation for running a successful non-profit through a year-long coaching process, eventually allowing these charities to successfully apply for grants and loans from others so they can further meet unmet needs in their communities.

Living Parables of Central Florida, a 501c3

www.ingramcontent.com/pod-product-compliance
Lightning Source LLC
Chambersburg PA
CBHW071735040426
42446CB00012B/2370